THE ART OF LISTENING

THE ART OF LISTENING

*Building Relationships
Through
Understanding*

AVERY NIGHTINGALE

Creative Quill Press

CONTENTS

CHAPTER 1

Introduction

In leadership and management, it has been said that it is time to "put the humanity back into human relations." Many of us find ourselves craving face-to-face interaction and opportunities to get to know one another as thinking, feeling, loving friends, family members, employees, co-workers, etc. Nothing is more rewarding than having someone demonstrate that they are genuinely interested in us and our ideas. These leaders and friends give us their undivided attention and make us feel valued. Would you like to increase your effectiveness in the workplace and your personal life? Do you seek a decrease in miscommunication and misunderstanding? Would meaningful interaction with family, colleagues, business affiliates, and friends build a strong, cohesive community? Are you one who might wish to be a good (better) listener, but you may have only guessed how you could become one? After 35 years of research and personal experimentation with this technique, I have learned that understanding is the key. What a pleasure to tell you that listening can make all the difference. Are you ready to see, hear, and apply common sense to the extraordinary power of intelligent communication? Believe it or not, listening alone can bring about the extraordinary in ordinary interactions.

In today's fast-paced and complex world, relationships have become more challenging than ever. What are the keys to successful relationships? How do we know if we are making a difference? Contrary to popular belief, I have found that the answer does not lie in global or national initiatives, high-tech equipment, or expensive programs. Surprisingly, it lies in something as basic as the art of courteous communication and the simplicity of building relationships through understanding. The most powerful tool I know is that of careful and skilled listening. It is at our disposal every minute of each and every day.

CHAPTER 2

The Importance of Listening

At the time of birth, most of us come with two ears, both in listening condition. But how many times do we use them to listen to someone and understand them? Many reasons are given about this, ranging from ignorance of the significant role that listening plays in our formative years to inherent biases and relentless denial of a free and positive atmosphere necessary for an active listener in us to awaken and emerge. But to accommodate the fast pace in which our living has shaped recently, we have let our listener go to sleep without recognizing its significance in our lives and relationships. We may say we hear what the other person says or we listen, but only sometimes our listener is active. What is the difference between hearing and listening?

We are all educated in reading, writing, and speaking by people in school. But how many of us get formally educated in listening? Not many. The ignorance of the significant role that listening plays in our lives is evident. Listening is the most affecting aspect of communication and relationship, yet the most ignored aspect. Not only that, our social behaviors are more specifically built on such communication skills as reading, writing, and speaking, and pay less attention to the art of listening. One dictionary defines literacy as the ability to read and write, and another dictionary adds the ability to do children's homework.

However, another dictionary defines literacy as having knowledge or competence of a specified kind. Evidently, listening is not specified as included in any of these dictionaries in defining literacy.

2.1 Active Listening

In any field of professional activity, anybody will tell you that the first and foremost principle is and should be communication. Good communication is one of the most demanded knowledge and most respected qualities in most developed countries. "Think about it: Most books and articles about speaking skills advise leaders/managers to communicate assertively, to build confidence in your role and show that you know and believe in what you say." Yes, interaction is taking place everywhere. However, despite all the inherent importance, nobody ever teaches us how to listen and I got to believe from personal experience in a firm that I was employed for quite some time that it is by far one of the most valuable communication skills.

Understanding and then being understood is the key to highly effective people. It is how you build relationships and establish trust, not only within your professional life, but also with your family and friends. Listening at work is the first step. That's why this article will focus on providing the basics to learn on how to listen. Having strong relationships can launch your career and make it more efficient, and less effortful. I will provide tricks and tips to capture and retain essential information from managers, employees, and coworkers through a lens of complexity or some hybrid model of self-development.

2.2 Empathetic Listening

As you listen empathetically, which includes picking up the non-verbal as well as the verbal signals, you may find your speaker making various mistakes of judgement, prediction or evaluation. However, as the listener gets more involved (and involved means making value judgements of a different order, such as those dealing with the experiences and feelings of the individual, rather than the thoughts and hypotheses of the individual), the speaker's own self-evaluations begin to gain expression. Thus, if you were evaluating a speaker's a priori evaluative, predictive, or selective statements, suspicion was created of your own motives; reduction of task-contrast or polarity was prevented, and the listener avoided the temptation to arrange the content of the speaker's field of awareness in a pattern of his (the listener's) own choosing. Schemas did not overwhelm presentation of materials, open and relatively undistorted.

Empathetic listening is the skill of understanding another from that person's point of view. This type of listening is beneficial to both the listener and the speaker because the open conversation initiated helps both individuals to better understand the other and also to understand themselves. The first step toward empathetic listening is to recognize that you are not the other person. Your feelings, thoughts, values, and background are not those of the other person. When you are able to recognize this fact, you can begin to listen to the other person as that individual, rather than from your own biases. This does not mean that as you listen you will not have biases or feelings of agreement or disagreement, but it does mean that you will be open-minded. Also included in this type of listening is empathetic understanding. When a person is an empathetic listener, he is able to put himself "in the other person's shoes," so to speak, in an attempt to understand the feeling of the speaker and realize the situation from the speaker's point of view.

CHAPTER 3

Building Trust through Listening

Part of relational leadership includes a vision for the group, along with values and relationships. Values can effectively bond together different types of people and provide a foundation for decisions and actions. In essence, relational leadership theory proposes that leadership sacrifices must be made by the leader for the benefit of the group. In doing so, the idea of working for the common good results. With relational stewardship, this working for the common good is rooted in trust, respect, teamwork, and steadfastness. Focusing on the group, encompassed by the leader, transforms the leader in such a way that they are genuinely committed to the best humanity has to offer, which ultimately manifests in the form of acting for the common good of all humans. Effective communication is another aspect of the stewardship role in relational leadership. Ultimately, from a relational leadership perspective, both listening and dialogue take place in the spirit of and for the sake of serving and empowering others.

Relationships are beneath the surface of what takes place between equals in leadership. In companies, institutions, and teams, leaders function as equals, although some may have titles that reflect more authority than others. Every person needs to feel that they are an equal member of the group, and the leader provides the environment and the culture for workers to form that sense of connection. When we interact with workers as equals, they subsequently trust us in our leadership, and we motivate ourselves and our team. Through listening on a deeper level in our encounters, we gain our workers' trust. Self-confidence, relational control, and conscious communication help "the bottom line" - productivity and success, and attain good interpersonal association between allies of good will for the benefit of the human community. Trust is fostered in the moments where a person feels heard and accepted, listened to by the person behind the CEO's exalted profile. It is then that a person says, "Yes, we can work together here."

3.1 Establishing Rapport

One of the best ways to avoid delving into very personal life with people you just met is through phrasing your questions to show that they can include their general knowledge on the topic, too. Rather than asking, "Have you ever been on an airplane?" which would feel generic to a seasoned traveler, say, "Do you get air sickness when you're on an airplane?" This question is specific enough that it's not invasive, and broad enough that the conversation can go a thousand different ways. Remember to distinguish potential rapport topics by asking open-ended questions, and then to restructure those responses into narrower questions that give you exactly the information you're looking for. Attentive listening will help you hear what words and phrases your conversation partner chooses to use, and selectively mirror those commands back to your conversation partner using careful diction that eliminates vernacular you normally use but he does not. This communication technique will help you sound like you are on the same page, or that you see eye to eye, even if you are quite different.

Remember, the goal of rapport building is to create, well, rapport. It is not to collect very personal information and keep it for yourself. Do not be the creep. For instance, it is not a good idea to ask your customer where his place of birth is if you sell office equipment. Your primary goal should be to build trust. They say that people are more likely to trust a company when the company documents they receive demonstrate empathy toward their concerns.

People love to talk and understand their own perspectives more than anyone else's. We can use these natural inclinations to our advantage, often by simply saying, "Tell me more about that," or "Can you say more about [specific topic you're currently discussing]?" To connect quickly with someone, to inspire trust, and thereby, to get better information benefits, ask questions and let the other person talk about themselves. Dale Carnegie says, "To be interesting, be interested." Other easy ways to start building rapport include using open body language, making eye contact, and mirroring your conversation partner's tone and energy. Remember to show genuine interest.

3.2 Nonverbal Communication

One aspect of nonverbal communication is the narrative function. In groups or meetings, some people act as though they are "in their heads," not "in the room." However, what we say nonverbally communicates: "God save me from your boring speech," or "I'm not going to be left out of the conversation, so I'm going to check my PDA." Students tell me they can tell when someone was attracted to them, angry at them, or interested in them just by the glare in the person's eye. Additionally, all this information is communicated in milliseconds, according to studies in the field of neuro-linguistic programming and studies of folk psychology. It doesn't rely on your ability to select the right words, really.

Hearing impaired people, or people who can't talk, can communicate in nonverbal ways. A smile, a hand wave, a shrug of the shoulders, a nod of the head, and touch can all communicate powerful messages. Even the absence of communication can send signals: the silent treatment, for example. One of the most effective ways of communicating information, according to some communication scholars, is nonverbal communication. David Zarefsky, in his article "Strategic Reviewing," states, "Our voice, our level of eye contact, our bodily orientation, our facial expressions and gestures communicate a great deal that even the best-chosen words cannot match."

3.3 Verbal Communication

Before leaving, let the other person save face if the conversation was emotionally charged. Give your tribemate a respectful "out." For example, if the opportune moment presents itself, gracefully back off by saying, "We don't have to agree right now" or if you wish to give the other person some space, offer, "I need some time to think before we continue this conversation." If you can sense that the person is shaking, their heart is pounding, or their eyes are damp, try, "This seems to be important to both of us" or "I didn't mean to wound you." These statements allow the other person to save face, reducing the likelihood of a further, additional blow to their self-esteem. Quell inflamed emotions. Making statements in a diplomatic manner should remind your partner that a personal attack wasn't the aim, saving your partner embarrassment and potentially reducing their vitriol, too.

Standing up for yourself means expressing your feelings, needs, thoughts, and concerns clearly, succinctly, and effectively without denigrating others. This can be challenging, but effective communication requires addressing any contentious moments with directness and politeness, reinforcing poor behavior as such without increasing its emotional appeal. Also, keep your focus. When the heat is on, it can be easy to stray off point or attack your conversational partner in return. Politely remind your partner of your point and avoid any cheap shots. For example, say, "Well, like I was saying..." or "I'd rather we stick to the matter at hand" or "There's no need for that kind of remark" or "I didn't attack you."

CHAPTER 4

Overcoming Barriers to Listening

Though it might eventually end up that there must be some underlying causes to any "less-than-satisfactory" issues afflicting the unit, some warrant must lie in people's hesitation or fear to espouse issues they believe the key audience would rather they avoid. Merely offering "open door" policies falls well short of the mark, readers might agree. You can go ahead and desist, but this doesn't change things. Regrettably, the balance six, paying up for nearly two-thirds of the populace, will not go to bat and express their standpoint.

Another common hurdle that tends to stumble all would-be Charles Schwabs is the resentment we harbor towards the speaker. More often than we'd know, we have been offended by the views of others and now it breeds a feeling that distills one's resolve to listen. Hence the best communication experts advise, get those feelings aired. Neutral position, heavily alternate is the zinger. A corollary of active listening is seeking things we can agree with. Listening is not a patch of land for toffs and coach experts. It is a right for one and all. Listening not only assists in grasping what people are saying, but what not as well. The "elephant in the room" dialogues are rampant in today's workplace. These are the secrets that suck up vast energy while most are mute bystanders.

Listening is not hard. Maintaining the focus to do it is. What hobbles us are the "listening barriers" that crop up from time to time, barriers that depend less on our ears having any defects, and more on if we can really overcome the predilection we all suffer from: self-absorption. By that, it means that when we should be following and trying out what was exactly said, we wind up as so preoccupied with our comeback, and in so many cases, wrapping it up before the other is even done! As if we were both under the spell of some ruthless time bomb.

4.1 Distractions

A person could also be interrupting or arguing with you while you're speaking. Once you give them the sign you're listening to them, they'll likely do the same. Avoid just waiting for your turn on having your ideas and feelings expressed when the opportunity arises. Whether you're interrupting, being interrupted, or arguing, run the risk of continuing a fight. After all, someone had to fight back, defend themselves, and confront the issue. The problem will exist, and the opportunity to remain bonded won't. At least remain on the same page with a common goal, which is to understand each other, and to show some sense of gratitude.

When a person you are communicating with is engaging in another activity while talking to you, you can end up getting only part of the message. Despite their attention to you, they may not understand everything you are saying. Not only could this be mindless multitasking, which doesn't lead to contributing successes for everybody involved, they could end up asking the same questions later. You could have misinterpreted their agreement as well. If their attention is anywhere else but on the conversation, just be aware of how responsive their feedback might be compared to yours. It shows that they do have other priorities, but at least they're making some sort of relationship effort.

4.2 Preconceived Notions

This post isn't about breaking down all the reasons we treat people unkind. It's about the reasons we need to listen. The start to anything is listening. Yes, there are some things that do need to be stopped by those empowered to do so but sometimes listening first can prevent these situations. Listening can change a situation when people just want to feel heard. I am not an expert on anything but relating with people. This post may have clicked because my voice was the one you were needing to hear, or someone thought "Emily is the rudest person I have ever known, maybe they'll read this." Thank the universe for either view. I sure don't know everything, but I know that I haven't been driven to insanity from lack of communication or lack of love. Use what you've heard and show a little love, who knows, one day it may be you who needs all the smiles you can get.

Most people have heard that it is important to listen without judgment. How often have we actually thought - well I'll try, but I already think that's wrong. Or we pass judgment after a person has left and find our opinion on someone is different once they leave. It can be hard to listen if we think we know what the other person is going to say or think we know what they should say. No one is in the business of truth provision. People know best what is going on in their lives. We can see bits and pieces through the lens of their eyes but so can everyone else. No one knows the things a person has said or done to other people to affect their current friendships, relationships, jobs, relationships. It is a hard sell to try to bring that about to make people feel understanding or empathy.

4.3 Lack of Attention

Several years ago, I wrote the following in a guest opinion in the La Crosse Tribune. I know that I still have a fair way to go before I can say that I truly listen all the time with everyone. It is something that is important to me and I continue to work at it. The divide between what people are saying and what they believe they are saying is often quite striking. I firmly believe that this has led to many of the problems that our society is currently facing. I would urge every single one of us – today – to turn off our cell phones, pagers, computers – anything that is a distraction (time wasters) – and to quietly sit and have a conversation with someone important in our life. I would further ask that your primary goal in that conversation is to truly listen to the other person.

It may seem like a cliche to say that the pace of life has increased. That said, I don't think you will find many people who will disagree. With increased demands on people's time, the ability and willingness to really listen has taken a hit. Most of us have experienced conversations with individuals who are, not so subtly, reaching for their phone to check a message, are involved in texting with someone else as they talk to us or with someone else, or simply seem to be daydreaming instead of paying attention to the conversation at hand. It's condescending and can result in increased frustration. The person not paying attention may have been the person who initiated the conversation.

CHAPTER 5

Enhancing Listening Skills

- Building strong relationships with others often involves understanding and helping others, rather than waiting for them to understand us. This principle applies to advanced level listening skills. This need to embrace mutual understanding is often represented by the symbol of a yin and a yang, complementing one another in the active process of learning and working together.

- In order to feel understood by someone else, we need to perceive them as responsive to our dialogue. In essence, when someone is truly present and listening, they will attend to the speaker and respond at the right time. To develop responsiveness and forge mutual understanding, focus on both verbal and non-verbal communication from others. This viewing of communication from the other person's perspective is about creating a comfortable atmosphere for those with whom we are engaging. We pick up on non-verbal as well as verbal cues. Posture, facial expressions, voice inflections, and dress might all contribute to our impressions of others and our willingness to communicate with them.

It's easier than ever to find ourselves listening while focusing on something else. It's easy to overlook someone's communication when we are working to meet a deadline, looking at our phones or being distracted by other thoughts. When we do this, we miss out on opportunities presented by others' expressed thoughts and end up feeling as though others devalue us. Conversely, when we feel engaged and valued by those with whom we are communicating, we are able to achieve a sense of understanding and being understood – both crucial elements of relationships. Here are some ways to enhance your listening skills in order to facilitate relationships through understanding:

5.1 Reflective Listening

Reflective listening is the most effective method of showing the speaker that he has been heard and understood. When employing this technique, the listener repeats (or paraphrases) what he has heard the speaker convey. The listener then goes a step further and offers a reflection of the speaker's feelings and meaning, not just the surface content. This demonstrates that the listener is striving to understand the speaker's perspective and creates an opportunity for the speaker to clarify and expand upon the thoughts he wants to convey. Reflective listening is the technique that is taught to professional communicators in the psychotherapeutic, counseling, and human resources fields to create trust with their clients and resolve conflicts constructively. It is especially effective when trust and mutual understanding are critical to a relationship. This is why in therapy, using the client's words is so important. Lord states, "Reflection leads to trust. Trust leads to movement." Reflective listening requires effort to accurately detect and convey the speaker's thoughts and feelings. It is a skill that may take many years to develop, and very few people become proficient at it. Although personal practice and understanding the technique is an important foundation for reflective listening, one of the most valuable approaches is to capture the opportunity to adopt it.

George Miller once said, "The major problem in communication is the illusion that it has taken place." Once we acknowledge this quotation, the solution becomes evident: open yourself to the other party, listen from the inside, and use a process to reflect back their thoughts with genuine interest to understand their perspective. This is the essence of the highest level of listening skill taught in business communication courses in the U.S., known as reflective listening.

5.2 Questioning Techniques

We can ask personal addition, which encourages the speaker to share a little more about him or herself. At the end of their stories, some participants tend to ask for our opinion or advice. The 'Can' I or 'Do' technique emphasizes the importance of hearing every part of what the speaker is saying. Asking someone to come clean since we are all there got released from the interest of what they are saying. Finally, there is also choosing and Contexting. This technique encourages a person with a personal message or a question to approach us. It looks like "You could say this to me" or "You could ask this from me the next time you have this doubt".

These are some of the questioning techniques that we can use to help participants realize that we are indeed listening to their stories. First, there is simple paraphrasing in which we simply repeat or use slightly different words in repeating the speaker's words. We can also use reflecting. This is similar to paraphrasing, but in reflecting, we reflect not only the content of the words spoken, but also the feeling as expressed by the speaker. For instance, we might say, "You sound so excited!" This tells the speaker that we know she is excited. We can probe for more. This is the technique where the speaker only gives a small part of the story and we solicit for the rest of it. The speaker might tell us, for example, "Then my brother went that day." As we drive the speaker to tell us more, we might ask, "And what exactly did he do after he got there?"

5.3 Paraphrasing

Instead, fill your paraphrase with emotion and affirming language. Sometimes when I'm coaching students (or businesses or individuals) who are newly learning how to effectively utilize active listening, I have them "paraphrase with flare". It's not a great phrase, but it sort of sets the mood. They might practice with a phrase like, "Wow, you must really feel overwhelmed by the number of choices you have to make, yet you are so excited and driven and eager to make a decision that is grounded in the reality of your dreams. How will you know when a choice becomes one that you can act on?" It may sound silly at first, but once someone learns how to effectively paraphrase, it becomes an extremely natural conversation tool that really fuels rich communication. It adds volume, depth, and weight to conversation, particularly during business negotiations or even personal relationships.

Good paraphrases help a person who is speaking feel as though they are truly being heard because their words and the meaning behind them are being understood. But remember, the goal is not to summarize. There is a big difference between paraphrasing and summarizing. To paraphrase, you need to shorten while maintaining the meaning; you cannot summarize. It's "Cliff Note" style listening. Summarizing is like a movie trailer – it sums up the content but really lacks any depth. So avoid phrases like, "So, what you are saying is..." or "So, you suggest..."

Listening in Professional Relationships

Listening is the most critical communication ability needed by maintenance managers who aspire to a leadership role. Hearing abilities may be typical and are seldom an impediment to professional success, but the difference between hearing and listening, and the amount of accurate information that is heard, understood, and retained, often differentiate average from the best managers. Developing a listening skill, then, represents an opportunity for many managers to improve. When a manager achieves a high degree of effective listening, others in the organization become comfortable, satisfied, and motivated. This opens the way to straight talk from team members who express differing perspectives, challenges, and problems.

Good professional relationships are built on understanding and trust, which can be established through open, interpersonal communication. Listening is integral to this. "The foundation of a strong professional partnership is the establishment of a meaningful interpersonal relationship... (that) gives all parties clarity, objectivity and purpose," according to experts; "...engagement, specifically listening, is the hallmark of these relationships." It makes sense, then, in the business world - where misunderstandings and miscommunication can compromise sensitive negotiations - we would be extra-attentive throughout, and especially during, high-stakes, critical meetings.

6.1 Listening in the Workplace

Many employees find meaning in work relationships. They also take great satisfaction in receiving recognition, respect, and reward as they work. Though some people believe others are at work to take all they can, most agree that we work for the same sort of reasons we want relationships. We need to belong, to have purpose, and to approach our lives with motivation rather than dread. In the best situations, we come to work excited about what we can get accomplished together and get there, resting easy at day's end because we have invested our very best effort. As we contribute, we learn, and we grow through the support of others who are trying to arrive in the same place at the same moment.

Coworkers who are good listeners are held in high regard by management and are often asked to assume leadership roles. When they do, research shows that their ability to engage others and implement plans is enhanced. Management is well aware that employees see listening as a valuable part of getting work done. It is no wonder that companies routinely set relationship goals that revolve around listening to each other and making decisions that include and involve all employees. Respectful workplaces are designed to pay attention to the varied ways each person can effectively contribute to work directed at a common good.

6.2 Listening in Customer Service

For the customer service professional, practicing deep listening has five fundamental tenets. Although deep listening has wide-ranging applications, we retain focus here on the overall umbrella of end-consumer customer service because certainly outward customer service professionals need to maintain a database of knowledge that can be both taught and also finite in nature. If there is an art to listening, it may be in helping others be listened to, proving a solid practice where the customer service professional works, in this case, to create a series of interactions. Of course, the outcome is that both parties get what they want out of the interaction. Even though the interaction might still be mainly a business proposition, there is more to business discussions if what comes from the interaction matters to the overall picture. With that in mind, the most important tenet of deep listening is the willingness to refrain from making assumptions about the speaker's message. Part of active listening could not be more true in the belief that messages can be as blatantly disguised as they can are honest. It is only the listener who can take a leap of faith in having faith they must come from a source that is very real, and how they apply that leap of faith is what then matters most.

We have posited a central thesis here—that whenever and wherever there are two or more people communicating, there is an opportunity for the kind of fascinating and mutually rewarding communication that we call deep listening. Of course, relational listening must begin with a willingness to be open to and interested in a variety of responses on the part of the listener. Perhaps nowhere has the art of listening seemed so crucial in recent years as it does in the area of commercial-customer communication. In the age of electronic customer service, truly hearing the voice of the customer requires that the customer service proactively assist in fostering a database of knowledge that engineers optimal systems that best serve customers. It also requires an attitude adjustment on our part. After all, there are, of course, businesses and salespeople as well as politicians who never seem to listen. The moral of this story? His or her situation and ours are really one and the same; therefore, customer service professionals who work in the business-to-business environment should look upon themselves as partners helping to increase mutual trust through strong alliances.

6.3 Listening in Leadership

To be an effective leader, a person need not be charismatic, deeply insightful or even a visioning genius. A leader, though, must be a listening genius. An effective leader must commit to the practice of deeply and genuinely listening to the members of his school, business or community. This practice often needs to be one-on-one. Without such a relationship-building pursuit, the illusion of leader as visionary, holder of great wisdom or, worse, the know-it-all or narcissist might result. Instead, the effective leader realizes that by using the very important technique of listening, she will better be able to enact helpful and support mechanisms essential to the ongoing growth of the members of her community, or followers. Such a practice allows the members to be themselves, to release fear and to develop high-quality cognitive thinking. With that freedom, the members begin to solve problems and to use their own creativity, all while being gently guided through their thoughtful leadership by the one they believe has earned their trust.

We have seen the powerful role that listening plays in all forms of interpersonal communication and particularly in today's need for relationship building. This may be no more important than in the work of leadership. Robert Greenleaf began a modern movement by removing the focus of leadership from the leader to the members of the community, employees, students or other aspects of a larger community. His concept of servant leadership was novel at first, but now has gained momentum in schools and businesses across the world. This examination of leaders who serve introduces the concept of "backwards leadership," the practice of a true leader simply following the lead of her members. How could one do this?

CHAPTER 7

Listening in Personal Relationships

To be viewed as a credible mentor, however, a person does not necessarily have to be an expert. Often a sounding board is enough-neutral and safe listeners who can be trusted. Another related story that offers us insight into what we call good listening features William Bridges, an internationally recognized leader in life transitions. This speaker, consultant, and author of both managerial and self-help books, often shares a compelling personal event that illustrates the power of really concentrating on another person. Being the listener has both long-term and short-term effects. The short-term gain, as Bridges' story reveals, is immediate relief of the other person's worry or stress. The immediate relief was in the fact that, for 45 minutes during the time of greatest duress, this manager turned his full attention to his employee, saying nothing more than "I see. Uh-huh. Um."

While much has been said about how the art of listening can enhance our understanding, that point often focuses on the workplace. But what about the significant and often life-defining interactions we have in our personal lives? This column provides some examples and suggests ways we can apply the art of listening to our personal relationships. Consider the case of Mark, a general manager in a large computer software company. He often found himself so consumed by the demands of his job that his children were the sole beneficiaries of the baseball games he occasionally attended.

7.1 Listening in Romantic Relationships

One of the biggest relationship problems today is miscommunication. Multiple studies have consistently shown that the roots of relationship failure are in poor communication such as interruption, combative responding, lack of partner engagement and irregularly packaged tools and interventions that increase effective couple communication (EQCC). Unfortunately, we do not have these tools (or at least the time) and cannot use them when communication is so rapid. However, we do have a second, sometimes underdeveloped but more accessible tool, the art of listening. Rash, Kerr, and Spero investigated listening ability and characteristics of the best listener and found that the best listener, regardless of gender, possesses high levels of empathy and responsiveness, and responds with spontaneously selected, directive responses. This, like other skills, is not one size fits all and has an art to it, meaning like any sensible protagonist, we must exercise constantly while understanding the nature of the relationship itself.

Have you ever wished that your partner would pay attention, listen to what you are trying to tell them? In relationships, our levels of listening may depend on the relationship, or what we believe to be the nature of the conversation. Studies suggest that we pay the most attention when we expect to be quizzed on a topic, meaning we may not pay full attention in romantic conversations, but we definitely don't in intimate casual conversations. This creates multiple problems in relationships. Due to the nature of most romantic relationship topics, we can't expect conversation to change and still maintain a healthy relationship, which means if we continue our same non-listening patterns the relationship will almost certainly fail and end.

7.2 Listening in Family Relationships

Accommodating one another. As you and your parents become busier with activities and schedules, life can become so full that basic courtesies become second place to your busy lifestyles. To build your parent-teen relationships, make time for the art of listening. Dr. Marshall Rosenberg, an essential voice in the communications field, reminds us of the importance of listening by the attention we are willing to give to others. The message may come through more clearly if you adapt yourself to the message. Dr. Rosenberg underscores the importance of listening to other people with your "whole being." In the presence of a good listener, people are often better able to concentrate and express their feelings. The listener's reaction gives them the courage to continue to speak.

Hearing is the physical process of receiving sound waves. In order to hear, your ears must be functioning properly. People are born with the ability to hear—and they often prefer hearing sounds or voices rather than silence. The only "effort" sound waves require is to be received. In contrast, listening is an art and a skill. It does not happen automatically. To listen is to consciously attend to the message and to work to comprehend what it ultimately means. It is in the meaning of the message, heard and internalized, that communication happens.

7.3 Listening in Friendships

Listening to friends is easy for some, but difficult for many. We may have to struggle against our natural inclination to give advice the next time a friend tells us about her troubles. The rewards are worth the effort. Think about it: people say to whom we're good listeners, "You always say the right thing when you're listening," as you contact the things your friend tells you that you promise to remember seven months from now. Am I right?

Often, we listen to our friends with only one ear. We're quickly ready with advice, all the right words, and even a little gossip that makes our friend feel better. Isn't that what friends are for? Some of the time, but that's not the greatest gift we can give a friend. Advice is for professionals like teachers, guidance counselors, and psychologists. Our most important job is to be a listener or, as I put it, an antenna. In our friendship, my job is to be there, ready to help my friend when she wants or needs me – and myself there asking her for help and advice. Generally speaking, though, my job is to turn up the volume in the transmission every time she says "yes" and the reception becomes unclear whenever she says "no." We have no right to tell anyone what to do, not even our best friend. Our mothers have enough trouble at that. Once in a while, when we become confused, we may even have to ask her to repeat herself.

We are friends because we sit back and have a good time together. Friends sometimes listen to each other's problems, but other than that, we don't expect to have to work at our friendships. That's why we enjoy them so much, because they're so easy. We can be ourselves without having to put on any of the masks we need to wear at our schools or with our families. With them, we can be ourselves all of the time.

CHAPTER 8

The Role of Listening in Conflict Resolution

Thus, the majority of disputes can be rapidly solved. More importantly, the introduction of next disputes (and a dispute) can usually be prevented. It is difficult to listen effectively in the throes of a conflict. Psychobiologist John Cacioppo at the University of Chicago found in his many experiments that a fraction of a second after learning of the arrival of the unpleasant confrontation, the human body in flesh falls due to the fight or flight reaction of the sympathetic fraught air system. To make matters worse, the response of the vulnerable fight or flight is actively responding to the furious or defensive blood of the reproductive air system in the non-verbal coordination of its mind (like calculating the point duties, the repair to people who would be) to make themselves more active!

Effective listening is required in every relationship, but it is particularly important where conflict exists. This is because a sensitive ear offers understanding, and if people feel they are heard and understood, they are more able to consider ways of positively managing their disagreement. Effective listening is important in managing conflict because it enables people to appreciate one another's perspective. When you're discussing something with someone and something comes up that you haven't thought of, and can immediately see "Oh, I know what you're talking about" or "I've been there and felt that way," it is very easy to see that listening is the key. If there were no understanding, there would not be a basis for solving a problem. Where conflicts are resolved effectively, they are mostly a case for listening by the staff personnel. This usually brings about discussions about the best solution instead of how each faction can win.

8.1 Active Listening in Conflict Situations

A major reason conflict is discomforting is that we cannot control the person who is upsetting or offending us. Because conflict adds significant stress to any relationship, all of the listening skills we have studied to this point are useful, but they are especially important now. One must summon his or her best listening competencies while discussing conflicting matters for at least three reasons: so that the decision maker may feel better about the process, people, and the decision itself; so that the message is not completely diluted by the emotion and is allowed meaningful consideration; and so that less disagreement or a limbic agreement can be achieved. Because we cannot always eliminate disagreement in discussing a specific matter, those will not be the focus of our guidelines. We use the term limbic agreement in our listening text to convey the idea of patching the relationship without change or improvement in the disagreeable duality.

Why are listening skills important? Active listening in conflict situations. We call disagreements that produce irritation, impatience, confusion, anger, and frustration conflicts. All conflicts are stressful; serious conflicts are distressing. All families and close relationships have conflicts. Conflicts are normal. They give decision makers feedback they do not want about the process or the decision itself. They expose irreconcilable differences about beliefs and values.

8.2 Empathy in Conflict Resolution

In the context of inter-group conflict, showed the positive impact of combining contact and cooperative learning in reducing prejudice and promoting harmonious intergroup relationships. Cooperative learning was found to have favorably altered students' attitudes toward the out-group beyond the positive impact of direct contact. Considering two types of learning, empathy-based and theory-based learning (feedback and testing) in a noisy context, show that students' collective behavior is significantly better with the empathy-based learning rule. In many experimental games, people act in a more competent or charitable way when they seek to understand others. Empathy proves to be a powerful impulse for both charity and for social connection in individuals and organizations, ultimately fostering peace.

Empathy is closely related to social understanding and is generally strongly correlated with prosocial behavior. In studies of prosocial behavior, people are willing to work harder to help if they believe that others are experiencing pain or suffering. Similarly, people are much more likely to help when they understand a situation as a moral or emotional issue, even though it might involve some cost. Empathy might in fact explain why, in a conflict resolution context, groups perform better than individuals. When decision-making groups go on identifying the existence of pain and adjusting to others, they can make better choices for the group as a whole.

8.3 Mediation Techniques

For those disputants willing to have a respectful conversation and listen to each other, transformative mediation might be helpful. At the heart of transformative mediation is the idea that while many problems have a solution, not all do; thus the goal should be on improving the quality of the relationship between the parties. The idea is that disputants are free to disagree, but not to disrespect each other. This type of mediation teaches very valuable and general communication and relationship skills. Evolving in part out of this effort alongside several others by other conflict resolution professionals and educators, Transformative Dialogue is more open-ended and less structured than many of the more commonly used facilitation and mediation methods. Assistants and facilitators try to stay focused on creating conditions for the disputants to listen to each other, "mine together" extensively for "new gold" together (solutions, understanding, win-win agreements, etc.) and then transparently evaluate those possibilities to help them find the desirable options that can stand the test of time and scrutiny. Qualified ESDR or Transformative Dialogue facilitator.

Another dispute resolution procedure you are likely to encounter is mediation. A mediator is a neutral third party who helps the disputing parties to try to resolve their differences. The mediator usually meets with the disputants separately to hear each side of the story. Each disputant may bring legal counsel if they want it. After this stage, the mediator then brings everyone together for a joint meeting and tries to help each disputant understand the other's point of view. The goal of mediation is doing what is in everyone's best interest. If an agreement is reached, the details of it are usually written down and signed by the parties, and those details are legally binding. Mediation can be helpful in that if both parties are ready, they may benefit from the opportunity to "tell their story" fully and finally.

CHAPTER 9

The Power of Silence in Listening

Truly understanding another must be pursued in an atmosphere of silence, generating those "full noises that surround us." For this, one needs the patience and dedication of the walker, who knows how to observe the surroundings with every attentive step, but without excessive haste. The importance of silence in the act of listening is an aspect that is unfortunately often ignored, considering how in our communicative dynamics, we are often forced into listening only for rational-functional reasons, for utilitarian and not for empathic purposes, nor for real human contact with who is both close and distant to us at the same time.

In this third post of our blog series "The Art Of Listening: Building Relationships Through Understanding," we focus on the power of silence within the art of listening. If one of the principles of listening is dedication and determination, in order to hear the other, it's important to know the extraordinary power of silence. One of the most important aspects of the previous posts regarding the estimable effort and dedication that it requires learning to listen well is that the skill of listening requires the absence of any desire. If I truly want to hear what another is saying, it's absolutely fundamental that I interrupt the usual flow of my thoughts or desires and meet with the other, that I listen to them. By doing so, I must also empty myself of my thoughts and opinions, giving the speaker my total availability, my interest and participation in the story or the argument, and not only in the final result or an emotional or rational satisfaction.

9.1 Silence as a Communication Tool

It should be no surprise that we have a great many health problems, emotional problems, and a great difficulty in understanding. We allow ourselves to content our fears and loneliness by participating in events. Until we seek out the real meaning behind the word or words with which we communicate, we might as well be saying nothing. If we make an effort to understand a path to a goal radically different from our own, we may choose to stay on our own course, but the understanding of the alternate route further defines the chosen road.

Speech and words are only one system of communication. Silence is an equally significant concept. We've taken a rather negative view of silence in America because our society values highly the ability to "make conversation." The chat so crucial to our social life is generally about nothing of much significance. Meaningful chat in our society is usually in conflicts. We pass up times when conversation would not be particularly helpful - use some other form of communication - because we pull away from the person with whom we would have communicated. No other animal on Earth expects training in communicating with its own kind. The animals have an instinct that keeps them close to their own kind in feeling and action. We possess an elaborate communication system but lack the instinct to use it otherwise than in superficial situations.

9.2 Silence in Emotional Support

The reason behind this advice is that people use conversation to enhance their enjoyment of being with others. And while political and controversial issues can stir the conversational pot, almost anything can be enough to get people talking with one another - from the weather, to the game last night, to what you had for dinner. But such talk is for its own sake - to help build our relationships. When it comes to emotional support, the apparent absence of silence can actually cost the listener the opportunity to offer the best. Rather than actively engaging the speaker in conversation, supportive listeners realize that simply being present allows the speaker to express themselves without fear of rejection or other negative outcomes and, in the process, decrease emotional distress.

Silence has an undeservedly bad reputation when it comes to providing emotional support. Caregivers often choose to actively converse - providing solace that is more like solace. Listeners might express this sort of feeling to the speaker. They will talk about themselves and their experiences, looking for things to say that keep the conversation going. These efforts, while well-intentioned, are misguided since they reflect our normal social habits rather than the norms of conversation with someone in need of emotional support. Research on social support indicates something rather simple to remember: listeners often offer the best service to those they care for by talking less rather than more.

CHAPTER 10

Cultivating a Listening Mindset

2. In that same vein – we have to be mindful of attitude. We have to dig deep and give up our preconceived notion of who we think we are and how we should be. We have to stop the treadmill of "I know that already" behavior. Know that you are willing to learn something, anything new. Anything unexplored. And if you cannot learn, you must understand the perspective of the individual. A listening mindset is a mindset of growth, perspective, and one that is adaptable to continuous change. Our mission is to cultivate a world where conversation and sharing become an avenue for re-learning and is a reflection of our ever-changing selves.

1. Listening to understand is about laying aside your personal thoughts or beliefs and opening your heart to someone else's message. With the goal of creating an environment of compassion and patience, your role is to be a safe space, a sounding board. Understand that everyone walks a unique self-perception of life and with this understanding, seek to appreciate and validate, just as you would have them understand, appreciate, and validate your point of view. This is a decision that comes from a heart of patience, compassion, and self-examination for the individual.

If we seek to be heard, we have to start by offering the respect we expect.

In the hustle and bustle of our culture, it often seems hard to find individuals that genuinely know how to listen. In a world where conversations have turned into debate competitions, listening has almost turned into a lost art. In our attempts to be right, to give wisdom, or to show that "we get it," we sometimes cut people off mid-sentence. Other times we don't fully hear what's being shared because we are preoccupied. Listening to understand is an art. Cultivating a listening mindset takes intention, effective effort, practice, grace, and time.

10.1 Mindfulness in Listening

In many ways, feeling the room is more important than reading the room because its impact and results are understood where words often do not go: the place that invites intuition not just to sense your immediate world, but the broader and richer world beyond language. These unspoken signs add depth and meaning to our leadership if we're paying attention to them. They take practice and discipline, like all things worth knowing. Here are some questions you should consider: What silences have I experienced today, and what have they said? What doesn't seem to be quite fitting in the conversation? What are participants' bodies telling me that might be in contrast to their words?

Listening is more than a skill; it's a discipline. To truly listen, you have to not only open yourself up to another person's ideas and their feelings, but also to process those thoughts and emotions without creating your own framework. It's an act that requires not just empathy, but what I have come to call mindfulness - first, in your own ability to listen to yourself; then in your ability to listen to others. At the root of all good communication is how we communicate with ourselves. If we can't bridge these internal divides, if we can't forgive and move past our own perceived limitations, we invariably bring that energy to our interactions with others. Only when we can find peace within ourselves can we bring peace to others. Truly mindful and artful listening is not just spoken words and dialogue - it involves silence, reflection, and intuition. It's feeling your way to understanding.

10.2 Open-Mindedness in Listening

Open-mindedness goes hand in hand with freedom of opinion, a human right to think, write and speak what one's active mind urges us to. We are all allowed to express our thoughts to one another, devoid of discrimination or revenge. Citizens of higher freedom democracies can in such spaces discuss and argue conflicting interests so as to generate common goods nobody would be able to achieve singlehandedly. Even in the most advanced societies, the exchange with a person who puzzles us, or who does not express concisely, is often this or that ungraceful. Do not reject outright however, or worse, demonstrate contempt, towards an out of the ordinary friend. The perspectives of, perhaps even the occasional joke of, the near-impenetrable opinion from that individual can stimulate us.

A truly open mind does not engage in interruption. Be receptive to a newly met person's ideas and opinions as long as punctuality, physical safety, and etiquette allow. Recognize that you do not know everything and that you cannot judge without real knowledge of someone's life and choices. Even if what you hear concerns a topic familiar to you, double check what you think in your own mind about what that individual means. Use the person's first and last name and your own name casually several times during the conversation in order to introduce familiarity and politeness into the communication. Friendliness is likely to emerge. By being open-minded and subsequently respectful of acquaintances when they talk, we contribute to building trust, better relationships and in the long run, better communities. Basing societal virtues on abundant friendships of respect and respect in understanding debate, we manifest strength.

10.3 Self-Reflection in Listening

Monologues may provide the opportunity for speaker education, persuasion, gaining decision support, or for listening information;

sometimes monologues become lengthy because the speaker is seeking clarification of their thoughts by verbalizing them. If a speaker continues an unproductive monologue, listeners must analyze the piety of the situation and determine if an interruption is warranted. For still other situations, internal assessment will be an essential factor in deciding the attention and evaluation needed for helpful invalidation of the speakers. Indeed, effectiveness as an interpersonal listener is contingent on the appropriation of the acts of self-reflection in listening, the deploying of corresponding listener-centric skills, and the mental balancing act of relational and task aspects of enacted communication.

Whether at work, in the classroom, or at home, it is important to constantly model our listening after effective strategies. suggests paying attention to modes of self-reflection in understanding personal listening tendencies. This two-stage process starts with considering self-awareness in listening. Active reflection on listening observations and experiences helps to promote self-monitoring, or recognizing when listening is effective and remembering how it was effective in interactions. The second stage in self-reflection during listening deals with action, or responding to our own thoughtful self-monitoring with actual changes that contribute to developing into effective listeners. The focus in self-awareness listening is about dealing with the overall importance of self-awareness in helping us to become more effective as interpersonal communicators.

CHAPTER 11

Conclusion

In closing, it is necessary for both professional and natural helpers to develop their listening skills in order to meet the needs of their respective survivors. By using the three skills of responding to silence, in addition to advising that Tomas (1978) has proposed, natural and professional helpers present themselves as open, warm, and caring individuals, which will be interpreted as indicators of being empathic. Employing Sollie's (1979) little "tricks" will allow helpers to see through the surface cues and look for the real messages, encouraging an authentic experience. Also, the end result may be just as beneficial to the helper in that learning to listen will yield a sense of self-actualization. With good listening, survivors are able to reduce both sets of their grief symptoms and feelings of loneliness, experience a rehabilitative bonding, and forgiving of the self. Although the therapeutic relationship may aid in a survivor's understanding of feelings, if their "self" does not experience personal growth, they may withdraw within themselves and adopt a superficial serenity. Based on both the Rogerian premise and the information imparted by the models and studies reviewed here, the increased openness to change in behavior, increased honesty, and a more active involvement in problem identification is measurable evidence that listening is more beneficial to a counselor than only intervening in a difficult situation. By fostering a genuine therapeutic relationship with survivors by exhibiting active and empathic listening behaviors, professionals are better able to serve the survivors' needs, strengthening their bond and trust in returning survivors to their optimal level of mental health.

If you can learn to listen skillfully, you will improve your relationships, including the one you have with yourself. By practicing good listening techniques, bereaved individuals report being able to work through the pain of their losses and become natural helpers of other bereaved individuals in their support group work and in their everyday lives outside of their group experience. Listening skills also allow grief counselors to provide caring relationships, which aid in reducing the grief symptoms of survivors. For individuals who are seeking out professionals to talk to, they may be expecting the counseling relationship to be the healing factor. Yet, when that professional chooses to listen and ignore their story, the counseling relationship may only reinforce their feeling of loneliness and despair. As Goff (1976) reiterates, "the common wisdom is that loneliness is bad for people's health and personal development, and people who are lonely often seek help" (p. 69) from those they perceive as caring. If the help given during counseling is judged by most survivors to be unsatisfactory, the professional has not done his job as a helper. Goff further explains, as helpers, we must practice the "art of listening".